WEST MIDLANDS TRACTION

ANDREW COLE

AMBERLEY

First published 2017

Amberley Publishing
The Hill, Stroud
Gloucestershire, GL5 4EP

www.amberley-books.com

Copyright © Andrew Cole, 2017

The right of Andrew Cole to be identified as the
Author of this work has been asserted in accordance
with the Copyrights, Designs and Patents Act 1988.

ISBN 978 1 4456 6459 0 (print)
ISBN 978 1 4456 6460 6 (ebook)

All rights reserved. No part of this book may be
reprinted or reproduced or utilised in any form
or by any electronic, mechanical or other means,
now known or hereafter invented, including
photocopying and recording, or in any information
storage or retrieval system, without the permission
in writing from the Publishers.

British Library Cataloguing in Publication Data.
A catalogue record for this book is available from
the British Library.

Origination by Amberley Publishing.
Printed in the UK.

Introduction

The West Midlands has had a long association with the railways. The City of Birmingham has three main stations, with Moor Street and Snow Hill being on the Great Western side of the city, and New Street being on the LMS side.

New Street was always the busier of the stations, and is still to this day one of the main hubs for passenger workings in the country. Most services that arrived up to the 1990s were changed from electric traction to diesel traction and vice versa, up until the advent of HSTs and multiple units.

On the locomotive side, there were two main depots in the West Midlands. Bescot, which is still open today, is located near Walsall, and is the main yard in the Midlands for freight workings. It is currently operated by DB Cargo. In years past, Bescot had a large allocation of diesel locomotives for local freight workings, but today there are only a couple of Class 08 shunters allocated to the depot.

The other main depot in the Midlands used to be Saltley. Located just outside New Street on the Derby line, it was originally opened in 1868 by the Midland Railway. At its height it consisted of three roundhouses, but these went out of use when steam disappeared from the Midlands. Saltley became the main shed that serviced diesel locomotives used on passenger workings out of New Street, and was also the main train crew depot. Saltley was the main stabling point for freight locomotives visiting the area.

The depot shrank in size over the years up until final closure in 2009. Today the shed building has been demolished and all lines lifted; a sad end for a famous depot.

Being in the centre of the country, Saltley would always be worth a visit as locomotives visited from all over the country. There was also a large amount of freight traffic that passed through the West Midlands; from coal traffic to Didcot and Ironbridge, to steel workings to and from South Wales. This amount of traffic meant that many different classes of locomotives visited the area – the main locomotives being Class 56 and 58s on coal, to Class 37s on steel workings. The Rover works at Longbridge also generated a large amount of automotive workings, these being in the hands of Class 47s.

Class 20s, 25s, and 31s were the mainstay on local departmental workings, with them working rail and ballast trains throughout the region. Class 47s and 50s were serviced at Saltley for use on passenger workings out of New Street, and most classes of AC electric locos could be found at New Street.

All in all, most classes of locomotives could be found in the West Midlands on virtually any sort of traffic, making the West Midlands an extremely good area to visit.

I hope you enjoy looking through my West Midlands Traction book, and hopefully it will jog some memories of some long-lost workings, locomotives, and depots.

Most of the older photographs were taken by my late father, Anthony Cole, to whom I would like to dedicate this book.

D3011 22 November 1981.
D3011 is seen stabled at Tyseley depot carrying green livery and the name *Lickey*. This Class 08 had been withdrawn in 1972 and was sold to British Leyland for use at their Longbridge works. It was eventually sold for scrap to Marple & Gillott, who scrapped it in 1985.

08068 4 December 1983.
08068 (D3083) is seen withdrawn at Tyseley depot. The loco had been withdrawn earlier in the year, and would be scrapped at Swindon Works in 1986.

08297 16 January 1988.
08297 (D3367) rests at its home depot of Tyseley. The loco also carries the number TS002 and has had its yellow on the front replaced by a pale blue, as it was only used within the depot. 08297 would be scrapped by Vic Berry, Leicester, in 1990.

08601 21 June 1989.
08601 (D3768) is seen stabled at Bescot carrying LMS black livery. Tyseley always seemed to enjoy applying different liveries to their Class 08 fleet, with 08601 being no exception. This loco was eventually scrapped in 2005 at Bryn Engineering, Wigan.

08632 2 December 1983.
08632 (D3799) is seen passing Saltley in the consist of a freight working. This had been overhauled at Swindon Works and was returning to its home depot of Frodingham. This was the way that Class 08s were moved at the time. 08632 is still in use today with DB Cargo and can be found at Mossend.

08694 26 December 1994.
08694 (D3861) spends Christmas 1994 stabled at Saltley depot. This loco was allocated to Tinsley at the time, but was outbased at Saltley. It was eventually reallocated to Old Oak Common, and has since been preserved at the Great Central Railway.

08920 9 December 1989.
08920 (D4150) is seen stabled at Tyseley showing signs of collision damage. This Class 08 spent almost all of its working life based at either Saltley, Tyseley or Bescot and was scrapped by European Metal Recycling, Kingsbury, in 2011. A life-long West Midlands-based loco.

09021 15 January 2000.
09021 (D4109) is seen acting as yard shunter at Bescot, looking immaculate in recently applied EWS maroon livery. Class 09s were rare visitors to the Midlands, but they did appear later in their lives. Despite the appearance, 09021 was scrapped by C. F. Booth, Rotherham, in 2008.

D8568 2 August 1991.
D8568 is seen passing Washwood Heath as part of a consist heading for Gloucester for an open day. Also in the working was D821 *Greyhound* and 47401. This is one of the only times I've seen a Clayton in the West Midlands.

20001 1 October 1986.
20001 (D8001) is seen stabled at Saltley carrying BR blue livery. The Class 20s were very common visitors to the West Midlands, largely due to the amount of freight that the region generated. 20001 was eventually preserved, and can be found at the Midland Railway Centre, Butterley.

20028 30 January 1986.
20028 (D8028) is seen passing Saltley with a departmental working while running solo. 20028 would be scrapped by MC Metals, Glasgow, in 1995.

20053 20 January 1986.
20053 (D8053) is seen passing Saltley double heading with 20060 on an automotive working from Longbridge, which includes new Minis and Metros. 20053 would be scrapped by MC Metals, Glasgow, in 1991.

25027 15 January 1985.
25027 (D5177) is seen deep in the snow at Saltley. This loco spent nearly two years dumped at Saltley following withdrawal and was eventually sent to Swindon Works for scrap, but it was scrapped by Vic Berry, Leicester, in 1987.

25035 8 February 1986.
25035 (D5185) is seen at Saltley carrying BR blue livery, complete with snowploughs. The Class 25s had only one more year left in traffic, and 25035 was happily preserved at the Great Central Railway.

25074 21 April 1978.
25074 (D5224) is seen at Washwood Heath with a very mixed freight. Withdrawn in 1980, 25074 was scrapped at Swindon Works in 1982.

D5229 8 October 1967.
D5229 (25079) is seen stabled at Saltley carrying BR green livery, but with a full yellow front. 25079 would be scrapped at Swindon Works in 1983.

25134 20 August 1974.
25134 (D5284) is seen departing Birmingham New Street with a passenger working. This locomotive had only received its TOPS number three months previous, and would be scrapped by Vic Berry, Leicester, in 1988.

25181 19 January 1985.
25181 (D7531) is seen stabled in the snow at Bescot. The Class 25s were associated with the Midlands all their working lives, with both Bescot and Saltley depot having them stabled there. 25181 was eventually scrapped at Eastleigh depot in 1988.

25272 24 May 1981.
25272 (D7622) is seen stabled at Tyseley carrying BR blue livery. Of note is that it still retains its tablet catching recess under the driver's window, which means the running number is at the opposite end. 25272 would only have two months left in service, and was scrapped at Derby Works in 1982.

D7627 2 October 1973.
D7627 (25277) passes through Water Orton with a rake of mineral wagons. This station has changed, with the impressive station buildings being demolished and replaced with a bus shelter. 25277 would be scrapped at Swindon Works in 1985 following collision damage.

D7628 3 September 1967.
D7628 (25278) is seen stabled underneath the coal stage at Saltley. This loco would be saved for preservation and can be found at the North Yorkshire Moors Railway.

25279 11 August 1986.
25279 (D7629) is seen passing Saltley with a rake of ballast wagons. Class 25s were ideally suited to this kind of work, but they would have less than twelve months' service left. 25279 was preserved and can be found at the Great Central Railway, Ruddington.

25325 14 August 1985.
25325 (D7675) is seen waiting to depart from Landore Street container terminal with a loaded working full of OCL containers. 25325 was used as a source of spare parts for the Class 97/2 'ETHEL' locos, and was eventually scrapped by MC Metals, Glasgow, in 1990.

25910 8 October 1986.
25910 (D7665) is seen stabled at Saltley. The small sub-class of locos were based in the north-west, and 25910 was renumbered from 25315. 25910 was scrapped by Vic Berry, Leicester, in 1987.

D5382 28 May 1967.
D5382 (27034) is seen stabled outside one of the roundhouses at Saltley, carrying two-tone green livery. Only a couple of Class 27 locos carried this livery and a few were based in the Midlands before all moving to Scotland. This loco was scrapped at Swindon Works in 1985 following fire damage.

D5413 14 May 1967.
D5413 (27047) is seen stabled at Saltley carrying original BR green livery. This was one of a number of Class 27s that were stored at Falkland Yard, Ayr, and was eventually scrapped by Vic Berry, Leicester, in 1987.

27059 2 April 1988.
27059 (D5410) is seen at Tyseley having been brought for preservation by Sandwell Council. It had been repainted into BR blue livery, and has since moved to the East Somerset Railway for a full overhaul.

D5410 19 May 1991.
D5410 (27059) is seen stabled at Saltley looking in a work-stained condition. The loco was spruced up, and appeared at Coalville open day the following week.

D5521 3 September 1967.
D5521 (31103) is seen stabled at Saltley carrying BR green livery. This loco was withdrawn very early in 1980, and was scrapped at Swindon Works in 1983.

31108 14 August 1982.
31108 (D5526) is seen at Birmingham New Street on passenger duty on a summer Saturday in 1982. 31108 would be preserved, and can be found at the Midland Railway Centre, Butterley.

31146 17 June 1986.
31146 (D5564) is seen waiting to depart from Landore Street container terminal with a loaded working. The loco had been refurbished, which included a repaint into original Railfreight livery, and also having a headlight fitted. 31146 would be scrapped by Booth Roe Metals, Rotherham, in 2004.

31159 1 March 1991.
31159 (D5577) is seen approaching Birmingham New Street with a coal working. Freight moves through New Street are very rare. 31159 was scrapped by MC Metals, Glasgow, in 1996 following collision damage.

31166 23 February 1991.
31166 (D5584) runs light engine past Washwood Heath carrying departmental grey livery. 31166 was initially saved for preservation at the Wensleydale Railway, but was subsequently sold to T. J. Thomson, Stockton, for scrap in 2009.

31248 26 July 1990.
31248 (D5676) is seen hauling HST power car 43151 past Washwood Heath while carrying original Railfreight livery. These moves normally included a barrier vehicle; in this case it was a former Mk1 BG coach. 31248 was scrapped by T. J. Thomson, Stockton, in 2000.

31276 12 June 1987.
31276 (D5806) stands at Saltley carrying red stripe Railfreight livery. This was another loco that was scrapped by T. J. Thomson, Stockton, this one being in 2000.

31524 9 January 1991.
31524 (D5575) passes Washwood Heath carrying plain departmental grey livery at the head of a short ballast working. 31524 was originally numbered 31157 and was renumbered 31424 when fitted with ETH equipment. It was further renumbered 31524 when this equipment was isolated, and was scrapped by Ron Hull, Rotherham, in 2006.

31970 16 November 1989.
31970 (D5861) is seen passing Saltley carrying RTC livery. This was renumbered from 31326 for use by the RTC at Derby. 31970 was scrapped at Crewe Works in 1997.

33001 24 April 1983.
33001 (D6500) is seen stabled at Saltley carrying BR blue livery. This class of locos had regular workings to Birmingham, and at this time were regular visitors. 33001 was the first Class 33 built, but would be scrapped by Vic Berry in 1989 following collision damage.

33015 2 November 1983.
33015 (D6523) rests at Saltley carrying BR blue livery. Of note is that the loco carries 2E in the headcode panel; the old shed code for Saltley. 33015 was scrapped by Vic Berry, Leicester, in 1990, having suffered fire damage.

33024 12 October 1985.
33024 (D6542) is seen stabled at Saltley carrying BR blue livery. This loco was withdrawn two months later following collision damage at Cardiff. It was scrapped at Eastleigh depot in 1986.

33025 20 October 1983.
33025 (D6543) is seen at Saltley depot carrying the name *Sultan*, and has also received a grey roof and red bufferbeam. This loco was later operated by DRS, and has passed to West Coast Railways.

33051 18 January 1986.
33051 (D6569) is seen at Birmingham New Street on railtour duty along with classmate 33062. This was the Wirral Withershins Railtour from London Victoria to Wrexham General. 33051 was scrapped at Eastleigh depot in 2003.

33064 24 August 1982.
33064 (D6584) is seen at Saltley carrying BR blue livery. 33064 would be scrapped at Old Oak Common in 1997 following collision damage.

D7076 6 May 1990.
D7076 is seen on display at Bescot open day, 1990. This Hymek loco is currently based at the East Lancashire Railway.

37009 2 August 1991.
37009 (D6709) is seen on Saltley depot carrying Railfreight Speedlink livery. 37009 would be preserved at the Great Central Railway, Ruddington.

37010 7 June 1987.
37010 (D6710) carries BR blue livery while stabled at Saltley depot. Class 37s were regular visitors to Saltley, and had many booked workings that took them past the depot. 37010 would eventually be scrapped by C. F. Booth, Rotherham, in 2007.

37012 22 July 1989.
37012 (D6712) is seen at Saltley carrying large logo livery from its days in Scotland. Alongside is another former Scottish Region loco, 47705. 37012 would be scrapped by Sims Metals in 2003.

37045 6 November 1987.
37045 (D6745) is seen at Landore Street container terminal having just been released from works overhaul, which included a repaint into red stripe Railfreight livery. 37045 was scrapped at Toton in 2003.

37051 9 January 2003.

37051 (D6751) rests outside the admin block at Saltley while carrying EW&S maroon livery. Despite remaining in service long enough to receive this livery, it would be scrapped by Sims Metals in 2008.

37057 and 37106 28 January 1991.

37057 (D6757) and 37106 (D6806) are seen double heading a rake of empty container flat wagons past Washwood Heath. 37057 carries large logo livery, and also the unofficial name *Viking*. Meanwhile, 37106 carries Railfreight Metals livery. Today 37057 is still in use on the main line, painted in BR green livery, while 37106 was scrapped by EWS at Wigan Springs Branch in 2000.

37059 9 May 1991.
37059 (D6759) is seen passing Washwood Heath running light engine in typically smoky fashion. 37059 carries Railfreight Speedlink livery and the name *Port of Tilbury*. 37059 is still in use today with Direct Rail Services.

37065 7 June 1987.
37065 (D6765) is seen at Saltley depot carrying BR blue livery, and also shows signs of collision damage – having had its headcode boxes removed. 37065 would be scrapped by European Metal Recycling, Kingsbury, in 2007.

37119 15 May 1984.
37119 (D6700) is seen stabled at Saltley carrying BR blue livery. At this time 37119 was just another Class 37, but as the pioneer class member it was assured preservation and was claimed for the nation by the National Railway Museum, York.

37175 12 October 2014.
37175 (D6875) is seen stabled at Kings Norton on track plant depot carrying Colas Rail Freight livery. At the time, this loco was on Rail Head Treatment Train duty, and was in top-and-tail mode along with classmate 37219.

37184 13 June 1995.
37184 (D6884) passes through Water Orton with a mixed freight, including steel and MGR wagons. This loco spent much of its career north of the border, and at the time had only just transferred to Bescot. 37184 carries civil engineers' 'Dutch' livery, and would be scrapped by T. J. Thomson, Stockton, in 2000.

37187 and 37229 14 December 1985.
37187 (D6887) and 37229 (D6929) *The Cardiff Rod Mill* pass Saltley with a rake of iron ore tippler wagons. These wagons were never common visitors to the Midlands, with most in use in South Wales. 37187 would be rebuilt as 37683, while 37229 was eventually scrapped by C. F. Booth, Rotherham, in 2013.

D6888 5 February 1967.
D6888 (37188) is seen stabled outside one of the roundhouses at Saltley depot carrying BR green livery, but by this time it had received a full yellow front. 37188 would eventually be saved for preservation at Peak Rail, Matlock, but has since been sold to Colas Rail Freight for a return to the main line.

37200 16 July 1986.
37200 (D6900) is seen passing Saltley depot with a rake of potash containers that were mainly used from Boulby. These wagons were an unusual sight in the Midlands. 37200 would be renumbered 37377.

37216 10 April 2002.
37216 (D6916) is seen stabled at Saltley carrying Mainline blue livery. This loco spent many years based on the Eastern Region and was a favourite of Stratford depot. 37216 was saved for preservation at the Pontypool and Blaenavon Railway.

37219 and 37175 28 February 2015.
37219 (D6919) and 37175 (D6875) are seen stabled at Kings Norton on track plant depot; both are carrying Colas Rail Freight livery.

37227 23 February 1991.
37227 (D6927) is seen passing Washwood Heath with a rake of loaded steel wagons, and carries Railfreight Metals livery. 37227 was saved for preservation and can be found at Nemesis Rail, Burton-on-Trent.

37259 and 37422 4 August 2015.
37259 (D6959) and 37422 (D6966) are seen passing Kings Norton while hauling a pair of nuclear flask wagons from Bridgewater to Crewe. 37422 carries unbranded DRS livery as it was on test following refurbishment, and had been renumbered from 37266.

37281 26 March 1980.
37281 (D6981) rests at Saltley carrying BR blue livery. This loco would be rebuilt by Crewe Works, and would be renumbered 37428.

37296 19 July 1984.
37296 (D6996) is seen waiting to depart from Landore Street container terminal with a loaded working. This was another loco to be rebuilt by Crewe – this one emerging as 37423.

37377 19 May 1988.
37377 (D6900) is seen at Landore Street container terminal carrying red stripe Railfreight livery. This had been renumbered from 37200 the week before, and would eventually be scrapped by C. F. Booth, Rotherham, in 2009.

37406 11 April 2007.
37406 (D6995) is seen passing Washwood Heath with a rake of empty container flat wagons. The loco carries EWS maroon livery, and also carries the name *The Saltire Society*. Despite being in service at this time, it would be scrapped by C. F. Booth, Rotherham, in 2013. 37406 had been rebuilt from 37295 at Crewe.

37419 and 20312 20 July 2013.
37419 (D6991) and 20312 (D8042) are seen at Wolverhampton while on railtour duty. This was The Jolly Fisherman Railtour from Hooton to Skegness. Both locos carry DRS livery, and 37419 carries the name *Carl Haviland 1954-2012*.

37422 5 June 1997.
37422 (D6966) is seen ready for departure from Birmingham International while carrying Regional Railways livery. 37422 carries the name *Robert F. Fairlie Locomotive Engineer 1831-1885*, and was rebuilt from 37266. This was a regular working at the time, and the chocolate and cream Mk1 carriage was also a regular on this working. 37422 is still in use today with DRS.

37501 7 March 1987.
37501 (D6705) is seen in the snow outside Saltley depot. 37501 carries its unique British Steel blue livery, and also carries the name *Teesside Steelmaster*. It was rebuilt from 37005 and would go on to be further renumbered 37601. It is still in use today with DRS.

37516 23 June 1987.
37516 (D6786) passes Saltley depot carrying red stripe Railfreight livery, while hauling two covered steel wagons. 37516 was rebuilt from 37086 and is still in use today with West Coast Railways.

37520 23 July 1996.
37520 (D6741) departs Washwood Heath with a rake of sleeper wagons while carrying Railfreight Metals livery. 37520 was rebuilt from 37041, and was scrapped by T. J. Thomson, Stockton, in 2007.

37601 7 September 2001.
37601 (D6705) is seen stabled at Saltley depot carrying European Passenger Services livery. This had been rebuilt from 37005, and was renumbered 37501. It was further renumbered to 37601 when in use with EPS and is still in use today with DRS.

37607 and 37409 29 March 2013.

37607 (D6803) and 37409 (D6970) run past Water Orton while on The Easter Highlander Railtour. This was a multi-day railtour that visited Scotland. 37607 was rebuilt from 37103 and was renumbered 37511. It was later renumbered 37607 when in use with EPS, whereas 37409 was rebuilt from 37270; both are still in use with DRS today.

37608 17 May 2015.

37608 (D6722) passes Lichfield Trent Valley with a Network Rail measurement train. 37608 was rebuilt from 37022, and was renumbered 37512. It was further renumbered 37608 when in use with EPS. It has recently been sold by DRS to Rail Operations Group.

37669 4 April 2002.
37669 (D6829) is seen stabled at Saltley carrying EWS maroon livery. 37669 was rebuilt from 37129 at Crewe, and is in use today with West Coast Railways.

37677 13 September 1996.
37677 (D6821) passes Washwood Heath with an acetic acid train. This was a regular Immingham-based loco move at the time, and it is heading for Baglan Bay. 37677 was rebuilt from 37121 and was scrapped by C. F. Booth, Rotherham, in 2008.

37685 11 February 1988.
37685 (D6934) is seen at Washwood Heath with a classmate while on an RMC aggregate working. This small batch of locos was outbased at Peak Forest for these workings. 37685 was rebuilt from 37234, and is still in use today with West Coast Railways.

37693 18 March 1987.
37693 (D6910) passes Saltley while hauling a rake of coal hoppers. 37693 was rebuilt from 37210 and is seen carrying original Railfreight livery, but has received large running numbers. 37693 was scrapped by European Metal Recycling, Attercliffe, in 2011.

37800 10 June 1990.
37800 (D6843) passes Washwood Heath carrying Railfreight Coal livery, and also the name *Glo Cymru*. 37800 was rebuilt from 37143, and has recently been returned to service with Rail Operations Group.

40001 25 November 1983.
40001 (D201) is seen running into Landore Street container terminal, ready to pick up a loaded working. 40001 would be scrapped at Swindon Works in 1987.

40028 7 September 1984.
40028 (D228) is seen stabled at Saltley depot looking a bit battered. It is seen alongside 56087. 40028 originally carried the name *Samaria*, and was scrapped in 1988 at Crewe Works.

40080 17 August 1982.
40080 (D280) runs light engine past Saltley depot carrying BR blue livery. This view shows the immense size of this class of loco. 40080 would be scrapped at Doncaster Works in 1984.

40122 9 October 1987.
40122 (D200) is seen passing Saltley depot while on an automotive working which contained brand new Rover Metro cars. This was the original Class 40 loco built, dating from 1958, and it would be saved for preservation; finding its way to York as part of the national collection.

D322 New Street.
D322 is seen at Birmingham New Street carrying BR green livery at the head of a rake of maroon coaches. This loco never received a TOPS number as it was withdrawn after only five years of service following collision damage. It was scrapped at Crewe Works in 1967.

40128 17 May 1981.
40128 (D328) is seen stabled at Tyseley depot awaiting repairs. With no main line allocation, Tyseley was, and still is, the main depot for the West Midlands DMU fleet. 40128 was scrapped at Doncaster Works in 1983.

40155 20 May 1984.
40155 (D355) is seen stabled at Bescot carrying BR blue livery, but showing signs of being spruced up with white buffers, handrails, and headcode boxes. 40155 would be scrapped at Crewe Works in 1988.

D821 2 August 1991.
D821 is seen passing Washwood Heath, being hauled by 47401 on its way to Gloucester for an open day. Also in the consist was Clayton D8568. D821 carries BR blue livery, and the name *Greyhound*.

44008 12 September 1978.
44008 (D8) is seen departing Bescot with a freight working. At this time only half of the class remained in service, with five already withdrawn. 44008 would be one of the last three Class 44s in service, and was preserved. Today it can be found at Peak Rail.

D137 3 September 1967.
D137 (45014) is seen stabled outside one of the roundhouses at Saltley depot, while still carrying BR green livery. The loco carries the name *The Cheshire Regiment*, and was scrapped by Vic Berry, Leicester, in 1986 following serious collision damage received at Chinley.

D14 21 May 1967.
D14 (45015) is seen stabled at Saltley depot carrying BR green livery. Of note is that this loco carries connector doors on the cab, which were only carried by a small handful of Class 45 locos. This loco spent many years dumped at Toton following withdrawal, and was eventually preserved at the Battlefield Railway.

45020 29 September 1984.
45020 (D26) is seen passing Saltley while double heading a passenger working along with 37003. This combination of locos was never common. 45020 would be scrapped by Vic Berry, Leicester, in 1988, while 37003 can be found at the Mid-Norfolk Railway.

45022 29 September 1986.
45022 (D60) is seen stabled adjacent to Landore Street container terminal with a sister loco. 45022 would be renumbered by the departmental sector to 97409, but would be scrapped by MC Metals, Glasgow, in 1991.

West Midlands Traction

54 20 August 1974.
54 (45023) is seen at Birmingham New Street during the period when the 'D' was dropped following the withdrawal of steam locos. 54 carries the name *The Royal Pioneer Corps*, and would be scrapped by Vic Berry, Leicester, in 1986.

45058 1 August 1986.
45058 (D97) is seen stabled at Saltley depot carrying work-stained BR blue livery. This class of locos were always associated with Saltley for many years, both on passenger workings and also freight workings. 45058 would be scrapped by MC Metals, Glasgow, in 1994.

45062 7 May 1986.
45062 (D103) approaches Saltley with a loaded ballast working. This loco had just over a year left in service, and would be scrapped by MC Metals, Glasgow, in 1994.

45112 24 January 1987.
45112 (D61) is seen stabled at Saltley carrying BR blue livery. By this time, 45112 had received a central headlight for passenger work. 45112 was happily preserved and has since been returned to main line use.

45121 4 September 1982.

45121 (D18) rests at Birmingham New Street following arrival from the south-west. Most passenger workings at Birmingham New Street at this time changed traction from diesel to electric and vice versa. 45121 would be scrapped at Derby Works in 1993.

D88 30 July 1967.

D88 (45136) is seen stabled outside one of the roundhouses at Saltley depot, having been repainted into BR blue livery. This scene oozes nostalgia, from the loco, to the wagons, and to the depot building itself. 45136 would be scrapped by MC Metals, Glasgow, in 1992.

45141 12 May 1987.
45141 (D82) is seen passing Saltley with a rake of DMU carriages. 45141 carries a central headlight for passenger workings, and would be scrapped by MC Metals, Glasgow, in 1992.

D139 20 August 1967.
D139 (46002) is seen stabled at Saltley depot having been repainted into standard BR blue livery. It would be another seven years before it gained its 46002 TOPS number, and it would be scrapped at Swindon Works in 1984.

46004 25 July 1975.
46004 (D141) is seen on Class 1 passenger work at Birmingham New Street. 46004 would be scrapped at Swindon Works in 1985 following collision damage.

46025 23 January 1984.
46025 (D162) drags a failed HST past Saltley, following a dusting of snow. 46025 was one of the last survivors of the Class 46, being withdrawn in November 1984 and scrapped at Doncaster Works in 1985.

46033 26 May 1981.
46033 (D170) is seen departing Landore Street container terminal with a loaded working. 46033 would be stored a week later, only to be reinstated for further use, before finally being scrapped at Swindon Works in 1984.

47007 21 March 1986.
47007 (D1529) stands at Lawley Street container terminal carrying BR blue livery. At the time 47007 was allocated to Gateshead depot, but later in the same year the loco would go on to be transferred south to Stratford and would be named *Stratford* in kind, which also included a cast cockney sparrow depot plaque. 47007 was scrapped by Booth Roe Metals, Rotherham, in 1994.

47060 16 August 1986.
47060 (D1644) is seen stabled at Bescot yard carrying BR blue livery. Bescot always had a large allocation of locos, due to the amount of freight traffic in the West Midlands. 47060 would later be named *Halewood Silver Jubilee 1988* and would go on to be included in the Class 57 rebuild programme, emerging as 57008.

47114 11 December 1994.
47114 (D1702) rests at Saltley depot carrying Railfreight Speedlink livery. This Class 47 was one of five locos fitted with different Sulzer engines and known as Class 48 locos. In the early 1970s, they were fitted with standard Sulzer engines, and were converted to Class 47s. 47114 was later named *FreightlinerBulk,* but was scrapped by Booth Roe Metals, Rotherham, in 2005.

47152 13 September 1996.
47152 (D1745) is seen restarting its Freightliner working away from Washwood Heath while carrying unbranded Railfreight livery. Freightliner had been in operation for just over a year, and they inherited many Class 47s – not all in the best of health – and most were replaced by new Class 66 locos. 47152 was eventually scrapped at Southampton Maritime depot in 2003.

47157 5 August 1974.
47157 (D1750) is seen departing Birmingham New Street with an express working to the Western Region. 47157 had only received its TOPS number the previous year, and would later in life find use with Freightliner, being named *Johnson Stevens Agencies* in the process. It would be scrapped by Booth Roe Metals, Rotherham, in 2004.

47201 5 August 1974.
47201 (D1851) is seen at Birmingham New Street carrying BR two-tone green livery, but with its TOPS number, which it had carried for just two months. At this time, New Street used to be a fascinating place to visit, with most trains that arrived requiring a loco change from diesel to electric, or vice versa. 47201 would be scrapped by European Metal Recycling, Kingsbury, in 2007.

D1868 21 May 1967.
D1868 (47218) rests inside one of the roundhouses at Saltley. Saltley depot would grow to a huge size, which included three roundhouses, but all three would be demolished and the depot would completely close to locos, with all track lifted. D1868 is seen having had its small yellow warning panel replaced with a full yellow front, and would be scrapped by European Metal Recycling, Kingsbury, in 2002.

47287 24 February 1997.
47287 (D1989) rests at Saltley depot having not long been repainted into Railfreight Distribution livery. By this time, the Class 47 fleet were used on automotive workings from the Rover plant at Longbridge, and were all allocated to Tinsley, but outbased at Saltley. When the Rover plant closed, all the automotive work ceased in the West Midlands. 47287 was scrapped by Booth Roe Metals, Rotherham, in 2005.

47300 4 July 1993.
47300 (D1594) stands at its home depot of Bescot, carrying civil engineers' livery. This loco was unusual in that it was originally numbered 47468 and was converted to a Class 47/3 by having its ETH equipment removed, and was renumbered in 1992. 47300 was scrapped by European Metal Recycling, Kingsbury, in 2002.

D1799 3 September 1967.
D1799 (47318) is seen in two-tone green livery outside one of the huge roundhouses at Saltley depot. Saltley was the major depot in the West Midlands that serviced locos for use on freight workings, and also on passenger workings out of Birmingham New Street. 47318 would eventually be scrapped by T. J. Thomson, Stockton, in 2004.

47347 13 June 1994.
47347 (D1828) is seen stabled at Saltley depot carrying Railfreight Metals livery. This livery was from when the loco was based at Thornaby depot, and it would be selected to be included in the Class 57 rebuild programme, emerging from Brush, Loughborough, as 57004.

47365 13 September 1996.
47365 (D1884) is seen departing Washwood Heath yard with a rake of brand-new Rover cube wagons. These wagons were introduced to carry spare parts from the Rover plant and, when the factory closed, most of the wagons were stored in Washwood Heath yard. The yard has since closed and the wagons are still stored in the yard, but most have had their bogies removed for use on other wagons. 47365 carries the name *Diamond Jubilee*, and would be scrapped by C. F. Booth, Rotherham, in 2007.

47426 9 April 1990.
47426 (D1534) departs Coventry with an Inter-City passenger working to the South Coast while carrying large logo livery. At the time this loco was allocated to Crewe, but would end its days on passenger workings out of London Paddington allocated to Old Oak Common. It would be scrapped at Old Oak Common in 1997.

47458 30 March 1985.
47458 (D1578) is seen approaching Water Orton station with a passenger working towards Norwich. 47458 was allocated to Stratford depot at the time – hence the silver roof. The loco also shows signs of previous collision damage with a new flush front fitted. 47458 would be scrapped by Booth Roe Metals, Rotherham, in 1996.

47475 14 April 1991.
47475 (D1603) is seen stabled at Saltley depot carrying Trans Pennine livery. This was the only loco to carry this livery, which was a shame as it really suited the loco. It would eventually find its way into the parcels fleet of Class 47 locos, and would receive the name *Restive*, but would be scrapped by T. J. Thomson, Stockton, in 2008.

47484 13 March 1986.
47484 (D1662) *Isambard Kingdon Brunel* passes Saltley depot with an Inter-City passenger working from the North East towards Birmingham New Street. 47484 carries GWR green livery – one of four Class 47s to do so, and all four were regular visitors to Saltley on passenger workings. 47484 can still be found in the West Midlands – being stored at Rye Farm, Wishaw – still carrying its green livery and awaiting restoration.

47488 15 July 1999.
47488 (D1713) rests outside the depot buildings at Saltley depot having been repainted back into original two-tone green livery. At this time the loco was operated by Fragonset Railways, and was on spot hire to Virgin Trains Cross Country for use on passenger workings. 47488 is currently stored at Nemesis Rail, Burton-on-Trent, and is a candidate for export to Hungary.

47501 7 November 1998.

47501 (D1944) is seen at Birmingham International station while hauling Class 442 unit 2418. The loco carries parcels red livery, and also the name *Craftsman*. It is still in use today with Direct Rail Services.

47530 18 August 1991.

47530 (D1930) is seen departing Birmingham International with an Inter-City working from London Paddington to Birmingham New Street. The loco carries revised Network South East livery. It had originally been allocated the number 47253, but was renumbered straight to 47530 from D1930, having been fitted with ETH equipment. 47530 was scrapped by EWS at Wigan Springs Branch depot in 2001.

47537 8 July 1986.
47537 (D1657) passes Saltley depot with an automotive working from Longbridge, which consists of new Rover cars. The loco carries large logo livery and also the name *Sir Gwynedd/County of Gwynedd,* and was a passenger loco at the time. It would be renumbered 47772 when in use with RES, and can be found stored at Carnforth today.

47551 8 October 1988.
47551 (D1746) rests at Tyseley TMD, carrying large logo livery. Tyseley never had a main line diesel allocation, being the main West Midlands depot for DMUs. 47551 was renumbered various times – from 47153, to 47801 and eventually 47774 – and would be scrapped at Crewe TMD in 2006.

47562 18 June 1987.
47562 (D1617) is seen stabled at Saltley depot showing off its Scottish pedigree, including snowploughs, Eastfield Scottie dog, and name *Sir William Burrell*. Saltley used to regularly get lots of visiting engines from all over the country and was possibly unique in this respect. 47562 is still in use today with West Coast Railways, but has been renumbered 47760.

47583 18 May 1988.
47583 (D1767) rests at Saltley depot carrying original Network South East livery, and also the name *County of Hertfordshire*. This was allocated to Old Oak Common at the time and had probably arrived at the head of a working from London Paddington. 47583 would be renumbered 47734 when in use with RES, but was scrapped by European Metal Recycling, Kingsbury, in 2008.

47595 26 March 1985.
47595 (D1969) is seen stabled at Saltley depot carrying large logo livery and the name *Confederation of British Industry*. This loco spent most of its working life in Scotland, and went through various renumberings – from 47268 to 47675, and finally 47791. As 47791 it would spend years stored at Saltley following withdrawal, but it was eventually scrapped by C. F. Booth, Rotherham, in 2013.

47596 1 August 1993.
47596 (D1933) is seen stabled at Saltley depot carrying the name *Aldeburgh Festival* and also revised Network South East livery. Despite carrying this livery, 47596 had by this time been transferred to the parcels sector, and was allocated the number 47740, but it never carried this number. 47596 was saved for preservation by the Stratford 47 group, and is based on the Mid-Norfolk Railway.

47602 21 September 1988.
47602 (D1780) is seen at Saltley depot carrying Inter City Mainline livery, complete with small numerals. The loco carries the name *Glorious Devon*, and looks good with the black headcode panel. 47602 was another loco to have many different running numbers – from 47185 to 47824, and finally 47782. As 47782 it was scrapped by T. J. Thomson, Stockton, in 2007.

47633 9 June 1986.
47633 (D1668) departs Landore Street container terminal with a loaded working. This loco was one of the original Western Region named Class 47s, being numbered 47083 *Orion*, and was renumbered when fitted with ETH equipment. It only ran as 47633 in service for five years – all in Scotland – before being stored in 1990, and was scrapped by MC Metals, Glasgow, in 1994.

47703 5 June 1999.
47703 (D1960) is seen stabled at Saltley depot carrying Fragonset Railways black livery. There were a handful of the Class 47/7 locos in use with Fragonset Railways, which were hired to Virgin Trains Cross Country for passenger workings, and they could be regularly found at Saltley. Today 47703 is stored at Wabtec, Doncaster.

47712 1 July 1999.
47712 (D1948) is seen stabled at Saltley depot carrying Waterman Railways black livery. Despite the livery, the loco was in use with Fragonset Railway on hire to Virgin Trains Cross Country for passenger workings. 47712 was happily preserved at the Railway Age, Crewe, following use with Direct Rail Services.

47726 21 July 2000.
47726 (D1626) *Progress Manchester Airport* is seen at Saltley depot carrying Rail Express Systems livery. Many Class 47s finished their lives working for RES, but when the postal contract was lost – and also following the introduction of the Class 67s – many were withdrawn from service. 47726 was scrapped by European Metal Recycling, Kingsbury, in 2007.

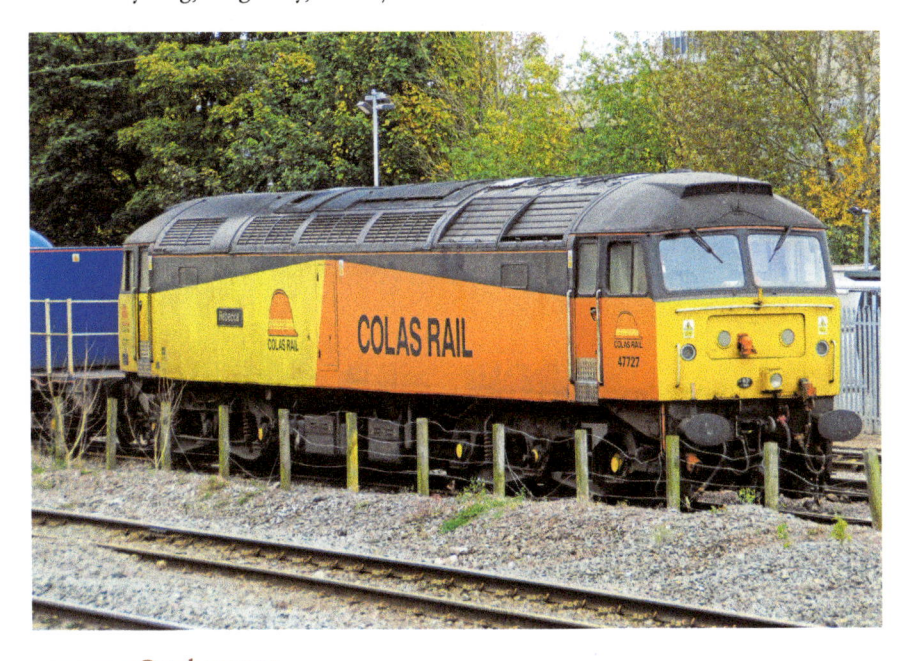

47727 23 October 2015.
47727 (D1629) is seen stabled at Kings Norton On Track Plant depot. This loco was in use on Rail Head Treatment Train duty for the autumn, and is operated by Colas Rail Freight. 47727 carries the name *Rebecca*, and is still in use today.

47810 14 September 1989.
47810 (D1924) works south through Adderley Park with an Inter-City passenger working. This had been renumbered eight months earlier from 47655, and looks good with a red buffer beam. Adderley Park is the first station outside Birmingham New Street on the line to London Euston. Today 47810 is based at Eastleigh, operated by Arlington Fleet Services.

47812 5 July 2013.
47812 (D1916) stands at Bescot having been repainted into two-tone green livery, and also carrying its original D1916 number. At the time, this loco was operated by Riviera Trains, and was being used as a route learning loco, but it has since been sold to Rail Operations Group and will be based at Leicester.

47817 15 July 1996.
47817 (D1611) is seen stabled at Saltley carrying Porterbrook livery. There were two Class 47s that received this livery; 47807 being the other. 47817 also carried the numbers 47032 and 47662, and was chosen to be converted to a Class 57; emerging from Brush, Loughborough, as 57311.

47831 28 February 1991.

47831 (D1618) *Bolton Wanderer* is seen carrying Inter-City Mainline livery at Birmingham New Street while on passenger duty. Of note in the background are the parcel Brute wagons; a scene that was so familiar at nearly every station, but has since, sadly, disappeared. 47831 was another that was rebuilt as a Class 57 – this time 57310.

47901 2 June 1986.

47901 (D1628) is seen waiting to gain access to the fuel shed at Saltley. This was an extremely unusual visitor to the West Midlands – the loco normally confined to stone workings out of Westbury – just to emphasise the point that Saltley was always host to the unusual locos. 47901 was initially used as a test bed for the Class 56 and Class 58 engines, and would be scrapped by MC Metals, Glasgow, in 1992.

47971 4 June 1991.
47971 (D1616) is seen arriving at Washwood Heath hauling Mk IV DVTs 82209 and 82224 from Bounds Green to the nearby Metro-Cammell factory, where they were built. At this time there were plenty of Mk IV carriage moves from Washwood Heath – both to and from Bounds Green. 47971 carries the name *Robin Hood*, and was renumbered from 97480. It was scrapped by European Metal Recycling, Kingsbury, in 2001.

47976 19 October 1997.
47976 (D1747) rests at Saltley depot carrying civil engineers' livery and also the name *Aviemore Centre*. 47976 had been renumbered from 47546 for departmental duties, and would be scrapped by EWS at Wigan Springs Branch depot in 2000.

50007 and 55015 2 June 1986.
50007 (D407) *Sir Edward Elgar* and 55015 (D9015) *Tulyar* are seen side by side on Saltley depot. At this time the Deltic was preserved at the Midland Railway Centre, and the Class 50 was still in service. Today 50007 is based at Washwood Heath, working for Boden Rail and is main line registered, while 55015 can be found at Barrow Hill. Anything could turn up at Saltley at any time, making it a remarkable depot to visit.

50010 19 August 1982.
50010 (D410) *Monarch* is seen waiting to depart from Landore Street container terminal with a loaded working. Saltley used to turn out almost any loco for container workings. 50010 was eventually scrapped at Laira in 1992.

50010 and 50048 23 April 1987.
50010 (D410) and 50048 (D448) are seen running light engine from Birmingham New Street to Saltley. 50010 carries the name *Monarch* and large logo livery, while 50048 carries the name *Dauntless* and carries original Network South East livery. Today both locos have been scrapped; 50010 at Laira in 1992, while 50048 was scrapped by MC Metals, Glasgow – also in 1992.

50015 11 March 1988.
50015 (D415) works south through Adderley Park with a rake of Mk1 carriages, mostly being in Network South East livery. 50015 carries the name *Valiant* and large logo livery, and was happily preserved, and can be found on the East Lancashire Railway.

50017 30 November 2015.
50017 (D417) is seen at Kings Norton On Track Plant depot. It had arrived to take two Class 47s back to Washwood Heath along with 50007. 50017 carries the name *Royal Oak*, and has been repainted back into original Network South East livery.

50021 19 November 1986.
50021 (D421) stands on Saltley depot carrying the name *Rodney*, large logo livery, and also a complete set of miniature snowploughs. At the time there were regular duties for this class to Birmingham New Street, which resulted in them coming to Saltley for servicing. 50021 was preserved and can today be found at Tyseley.

50026 27 July 1982. 50026 (D426) is seen passing Water Orton heading north on a passenger working. This loco was refurbished at Doncaster Works in the autumn of 1982, so could possibly be heading north for this. 50026 carries the name *Indomitable*, and was sold for scrap to Booth Roe Metals, Rotherham. Happily, it escaped the yard to be preserved, and can be found today at Eastleigh Works.

50050 3 May 2016. 50050 (D400) passes Longbridge turn back sidings along with 50007 and 47749. The locos were returning to Washwood Heath, having been on display at St Phillips Marsh open day. 50050 carries the name *Fearless*, and was the first Class 50 built.

D1047 20 August 1974. D1047 *Western Lord* is seen at Birmingham New Street waiting to depart for London Paddington. Very much in the twilight of its career, D1047 was scrapped at Swindon Works in 1976.

D9009 2 May 2013. D9009 (55009) *Alycidon* is seen powering through Water Orton with a light engine move from Barrow Hill to Swanage, hauling 33108, 55019 *Royal Highland Fusilier* and 37521. Always nice to see Deltics on the main line, but to get two in one move was great.

55015 2 June 1986. 55015 (D9015) is seen stabled at Saltley depot while preserved. The loco carries the name *Tulyar* and had been on display at Coalville open day the previous day and was then on its way to Ashford for their open day the following week. At the time the loco was based at the Midland Railway Centre, but today can be found at Barrow Hill.

D9000 19 June 1999. D9000 (55022) *Royal Scots Grey* is seen at Birmingham New Street carrying original green livery. During the summer of 1999, D9000 was hired to Virgin Trains Cross Country for Saturday workings to Ramsgate.

55022 19 June 2012.
55022 (D9000) pauses at Walsall with a light engine move from Bishop's Lydyard on the West Somerset Railway, to Crewe; the loco is hauling just a single Mk1 coach. 55022 carries the name *Royal Scots Grey*, and is currently on hire to GBRf.

56023 16 November 1991.
A view that shows just how busy Washwood Heath used to be, with 56023 in the centre on an MGR working to Didcot Power Station. Also in the view are 47310, 31113 and 58014. 56023 would eventually be scrapped by Booth Roe Metals, Rotherham, in 2004.

56026 9 July 1988.
56026 stands at Saltley depot still carrying BR blue livery. This Class 56 never received a repaint – being withdrawn carrying BR blue – and was scrapped by Booth Roe Metals, Rotherham, in 1996.

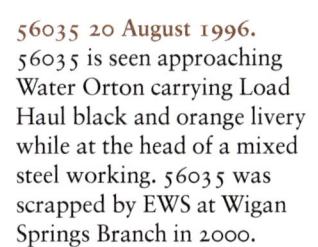

56035 20 August 1996.
56035 is seen approaching Water Orton carrying Load Haul black and orange livery while at the head of a mixed steel working. 56035 was scrapped by EWS at Wigan Springs Branch in 2000.

56068 27 February 1991.
56068 passes through Washwood Heath with a loaded MGR working to Didcot Power Station while carrying red stripe Railfreight livery. 56068 was eventually scrapped by European Metal Recycling, Kingsbury, in 2010.

56078 1 April 2004.
56078 *Doncaster Enterprise* is seen on Saltley depot the day after it had been withdrawn from EWS service, being the last member of the class in service. 56078 had been returned to large logo livery and looked superb. It would go on to be used in France by Fertis before returning to the UK and being sold to Colas Rail Freight; returning to the main line.

56103 3 February 2015.
56103 passes through Coleshill Parkway running light engine. The loco carries former Fertis livery, and is currently operated by BAR (British American Railway).

56113 15 February 2016.
56113 is seen running through Water Orton in Colas Rail Freight livery, while hauling 60087 towards Washwood Heath. 56113 was one of the class that worked in France for Fertis on high-speed line construction workings.

56311, 56051, 56018 and 56060 17 January 2013.
56311 (56057) is seen at Water Orton while hauling sister locos 56051, 56018 and 56060 from Nemesis Rail at Burton-on-Trent to Washwood Heath. 56311 was renumbered from 56057 and carries DCR (Devon and Cornwall Railway) livery, while the three dead locos all carry Fertis livery, having been used in France on high speed line construction workings.

57007 7 July 2014.
57007 (D1813) is seen at Bescot carrying Direct Rail Services livery. This class of twelve locos were rebuilt from Class 47 locos – this one from 47332 – and all were initially used by Freightliner, before most of them finding use with DRS. Today most are now stored at MOD Longtown.

57012 7 March 2007.
57012 (D1790) *Freightliner Envoy* is seen passing Washwood Heath with a loaded container working. This loco was rebuilt from 47309 at Brush Loughborough, and is today stored at MOD Longtown, having last worked for Direct Rail Services.

58006 1 August 1984.
58006 is seen at Saltley depot having not long been released to traffic and is seen on crew training duty while carrying red stripe Railfreight livery. 58006 would eventually be sent to France for high-speed construction workings, and is currently stored at Alizay depot, Rouen, awaiting a decision on its future along with another twenty-two members of the class.

59206 13 November 1999.
59206 is seen at Washwood Heath while of an aggregate working from the nearby RMC factory. The Class 59s have never been common visitors to the Midlands, and I think this working was a one off. 59206 carries the name *Pride of Ferrybridge*.

60020 17 April 2013.
60020 passes Washwood Heath while working 6E41 – the 11.10 a.m. Westerleigh to Lindsey oil working – while carrying DB Schenker livery. Today this working doesn't run, and the gasholders in the background have been dismantled.

67010 30 October 2014.
67010 stands at Birmingham Moor Street having arrived on a Chiltern Mainline working from London Marylebone. The loco carries former Wrexham & Shropshire livery, and after use with W&S, it found employment with Chiltern. Today this loco carries Caledonian Sleeper livery, and the Class 67s have been replaced with Class 68s on the Chiltern Mainline workings.

73106 23 May 1985.
73106 (E6012) is seen stabled at Saltley depot carrying BR blue livery. This class of loco were incredibly rare visitors to the Midlands, and in BR days their visits could be counted on one hand. Not sure what brought this electro-diesel to Saltley, but it disappeared back south not long after. 73106 was scrapped by Booth Roe Metals, Rotherham, in 2004.

81008 31 July 1982.
81008 (E3010) is seen on one of the centre roads at Birmingham New Street carrying BR blue livery, complete with domino headcode panel. Many services at New Street at this time changed from electric to diesel traction and vice versa. 81008 was scrapped by Coopers Metals, Sheffield, in 1991.

E3011 20 August 1974.
E3011 (81009) is seen at Birmingham New Street while still carrying its pre-TOPS number of E3011. 81009 would be scrapped by Coopers Metals, Sheffield, in 1992, along with most members of the class.

82004 14 August 1982.
82004 (E3050) stands at Birmingham New Street at the head of a rake of Mk1 carriages. There were ten of these locos built and one survives today in preservation. 82004 was scrapped by Vic Berry, Leicester, in 1984.

83010 14 August 1982.
83010 (E3033) is seen carrying BR blue livery at Birmingham New Street. This loco would take over from a diesel, and would work towards the North West. 83010 would eventually be scrapped by Vic Berry, Leicester, in 1984.

83012 19 July 1975.
83012 (E3035) is seen at Birmingham New Street while still retaining its headcode blinds. This loco would be the sole survivor of the class – happily being preserved – and can today be found at Barrow Hill.

85005 18 April 1987.
85005 (E3060) is seen stabled at Bescot surrounded by Class 58 locos. Bescot was primarily a diesel stabling point, but AC electrics also visited for stabling while on freight duty. 85005 was scrapped by MC Metals, Glasgow, in 1993.

85025 9 July 1988.
85025 (E3080) is seen inside Tyseley depot while undergoing repairs. There were no main line locos allocated to Tyseley – the depot being the main hub for the West Midlands DMU fleet; although both diesel and electric locos visited for repairs. 85025 would be scrapped by Vic Berry, Leicester, in 1990.

85034 27 January 1990.
85034 (E3089) is seen at Birmingham New Street having arrived with a passenger working. It has been uncoupled, and is stabling ready to work back to the north. This was the last year for 85034 to be in service – being withdrawn ten months later – and it was scrapped by MC Metals, Glasgow, in 1993.

86206 29 March 1991.
86206 (E3184) *City of Stoke-on-Trent* is seen at Birmingham International with an Inter-City working to London Euston. The consist has a parcels liveried Mk1 BG carriage in place of the Mk3 DVT. 86206 would be scrapped by Sims Metals at Caerwent in 2004.

86244 1 July 1991.
86244 (E3178) is seen being hauled through Washwood Heath with an Inter-City working from Birmingham New Street to London Euston. This was a regular move when there were problems with the overhead wires, with the loco and stock diesel-hauled from New Street to Nuneaton. 86244 carries the name *The Royal British-Legion*, and would be scrapped at Immingham Railfreight Terminal in 2003.

86256 31 July 1982.
86256 (E3135) *Pebble Mill* is seen at Birmingham New Street at the head of an Inter-City working, while still carrying BR blue livery. Of note are the parcels being loaded into the Mk1 BG coach – an everyday scene at the time. 86256 was scrapped by Ron Hull, Rotherham, in 2006.

87003 25 July 1975.
87003 is seen in original condition at Birmingham New Street. This view shows the running numbers on both cabs, and the BR double arrow placed in the centre of the bodyside. It would later be named *Patriot*, and was eventually exported to Bulgaria in 2009.

90016 14 September 1989.
90016 is seen passing through Adderley Park on the final approach to Birmingham New Street with an Inter-City working from London Euston. The line to the right has since been lifted, and 90016 now carries Freightliner green livery.

92031 6 June 2001.
92031 is seen stabled at Saltley depot, having been repainted at Toton into EWS maroon livery. The loco would be named the following week as *The Institute of Logistics and Transport*. With no overhead wires, the numbers of AC loco visitors to Saltley can be counted on one hand, with the only other loco I know of being 86426 – again, on its way to Toton for repainting.

97303 and 97304 4 February 2016.
97303 (D6878) and 97304 (D6917) are seen stabled at Bescot carrying Network Rail yellow livery. Both of these locos were on ballast duty for the Cambrian line, and were both renumbered from Class 37 locos; 97303 from 37178, while 97304 was renumbered from 37217. There are four of these locos in use with Network Rail.

97406 7 March 1987.
97406 (D335) is seen stabled at Tyseley depot carrying BR blue livery. This loco was withdrawn at the time; its use as a departmental loco used in connection with the Crewe station remodelling having been completed. It would be restored to BR green livery at Tyseley, and would be preserved at the East Lancashire Railway.

51189 21 June 1986.
51189 is seen stabled on Tyseley DMU depot carrying BR blue and grey livery. This vehicle was built by Metro-Cammell and was classified as a Class 101 car. Preserved, it can be found on the Keighley and Worth Valley Railway.

51272 22 February 1986.
51272 is seen stabled at Tyseley carrying BR blue livery coupled with sister car 54443. This Class 105 set was based at Norwich at the time, and would have worked to Birmingham via Peterborough. Car 51272 was scrapped by Mayer Newman, Snailwell, in February 1987.

304006 5 May 1984.
304006 is seen making a station call at Bescot with a working towards Birmingham New Street. Of note is the fact that the station has yet to be renamed Bescot Stadium, and that the Class 304 still retained its four carriages; the middle trailer car has yet to be removed to make a three-car set. There are no Class 304s left, with all forty-five sets being scrapped.

310060 14 September 1989.
310060 departs Adderley Park with a stopping service to Birmingham New Street. For many years the Class 310 units operated stopping services between Birmingham and London, until they were replaced by Class 317s and Class 321s. Some were converted to Class 310/1s, and all the Class 310/0s were transferred to East Ham for use out of London Fenchurch Street.

65444 12 April 1986.
65444 is seen at Tyseley, having come down from Bury to use the wheel lathe. The Class 504 units ran on 1,200v DC, and so had to be hauled from Manchester. They were eventually replaced by the Manchester Metrolink system, with all but one set being scrapped; including 65444, which was scrapped by MC Metals, Glasgow, in 1991.